Contents

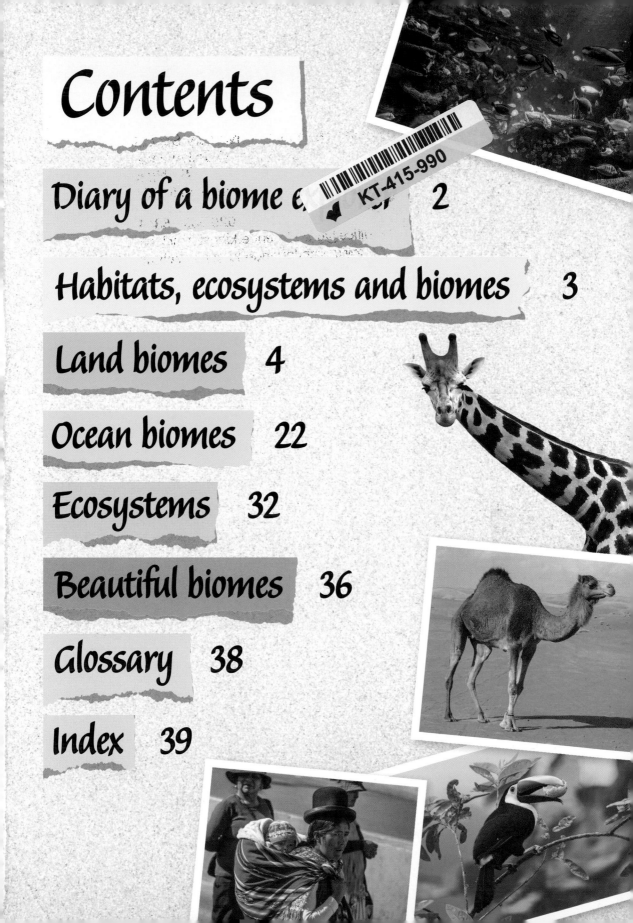

Diary of a biome explorer

14th June, Home

I'm off to explore some of our planet's **biomes**. A biome means all the living things in a particular environment, such as a desert. I'll visit the main land ones and some ocean biomes to see how animals, plants and people **adapt** to their **environments**.

Orangutans, land biome, tropical rainforest

Humpback whale, open ocean biome

Sami people, land biome, tundra

Habitats, ecosystems and biomes

Our planet Earth is not the same all over. Each place has its own environment, with its own usual temperatures, amounts of water and light, and types of soil and rock.

The toucan's **habitat** is the **tropical** rainforest.

A **habitat** is a place where a particular type of plant or animal lives. Plants and animals adapt to survive in their habitat and its environment. Many different types of plants and animals can live in the same habitat.

An **ecosystem** is all the life in a particular environment. It can be great or small – an ocean, a pond or a puddle! Really big ecosystems, or collections of ecosystems, are called biomes.

Land biomes

Mediterranean scrub

15th June, Home

I've packed for all weathers because my journey will take me through different **climate zones**. These are the ten land biomes I'm visiting:

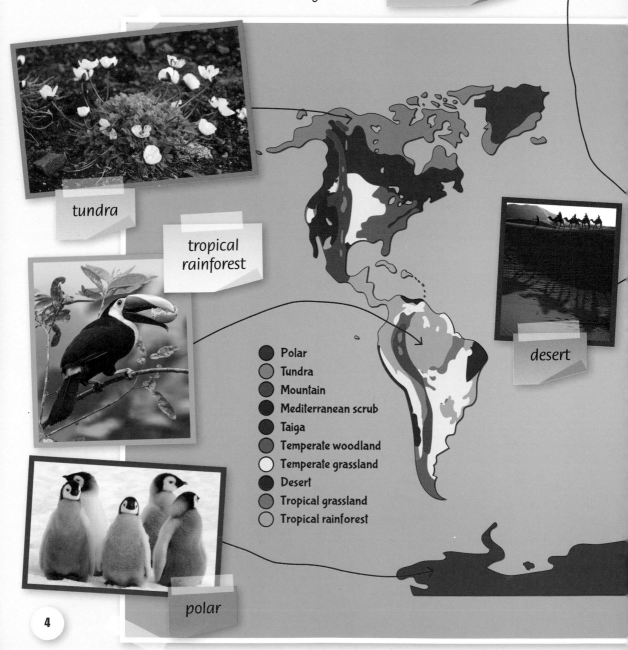

tundra

tropical rainforest

desert

- Polar
- Tundra
- Mountain
- Mediterranean scrub
- Taiga
- Temperate woodland
- Temperate grassland
- Desert
- Tropical grassland
- Tropical rainforest

polar

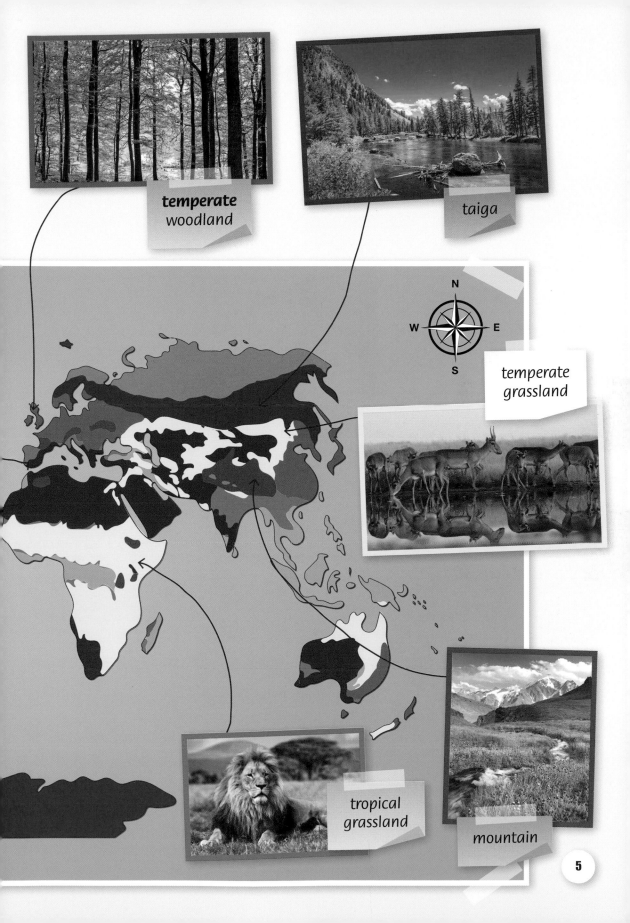

temperate woodland

taiga

temperate grassland

tropical grassland

mountain

Polar biome

Description:
Ice-covered regions around the North and South Poles

16th June, North Pole

I'm at the North Pole. There's snow and ice everywhere – and it's like this all-year round. Brrrr! Polar bears hunt here as well as further south, in the tundra. I'm heading there next.

The polar bear has thick fur and a layer of fat called blubber to keep in body heat.

ECO ALERT!

Global warming is affecting the rate at which ice melts at the polar regions and this melted ice makes the sea waters rise. This means that some coastal places often thousands of kilometres from the Polar regions are flooded and covered by the sea.

Tundra biome

Description:
Very cold, treeless plains
on frozen ground just
below the Arctic

23rd June, Finland

Here in the tundra biome, the
average winter temperature
is −28 °C. It's summer now so
there's no snow, but the soil
is frozen. My guide explained
that's why there are no trees.
There are only tough,
low-growing plants such as
moss, lichen and grass.

Tundra plants

The Sami people live in the
Arctic, in the far north of
Norway, Sweden, Finland and
parts of Russia. Most Sami
people live in towns now, but
a few follow a traditional way
of life. They herd reindeer,
eat reindeer meat and drink
reindeer milk. They use the
animals' skins to make clothes
and tents.

PLEASED TO
MEET YOU

Taiga biome

Description:

Northern conifer forests that have very cold, long winters and mild summers

30th June, USA

I'm in Yellowstone Park. It's part of the taiga – a forest biome that stretches across the far north of North America, Europe and Asia. Summers are short here and winters are bitterly cold. All the trees are firs, pines and other conifers. The ground is soft and spongy because of all the fallen pine needles. Moss and lichen grow here, too.

Pine cone

Needles are tough. They can cope with freezing temperatures.

Staying alive

These animals have all adapted to live in the taiga biome.

GREAT HORNED OWL

Adapted to survive

o has keen hearing so can detect small mammals under the snow to hunt

BROWN BEAR

Adapted to survive

o hibernates in winter to avoid the cold

MOOSE

Adapted to survive

o can eat and digest pine and spruce needles

WEASEL

Adapted to survive

o has a white coat in winter for camouflage to protect it from **predators** that hunt it

Temperate woodland biome

Description:

Woods that have cold winters and short, cool summers

7th July, UK

I'm in England to explore the temperate woodland biome. Oak, beech and chestnut trees grow here. They are deciduous – they lose their leaves in autumn and grow new ones in spring.

In spring, when sunshine reaches the forest floor, flowers bloom!

Woodpeckers peck out a nest hole to raise their chicks.

Temperate woodland life

Red squirrel

ECO ALERT!

Most British woodlands don't have **native** red squirrels any more. Grey squirrels brought from North America have taken over. Red squirrels can only eat acorns when they're ripe, but greys can eat unripe ones. Therefore, grey squirrels eat the acorns first, and there is no food left for red squirrels.

Grey squirrel

The Cherokee people used to live in the temperate woodland biome in south-eastern USA. They grew squash and other vegetables in forest clearings. They also hunted deer, rabbits and wild turkeys, and gathered acorns, chestnuts and berries.

Traditional Cherokee homes were built from young trees covered in mud.

PLEASED TO MEET YOU

Mountain biome

Description:

A mound of high ground, usually taller than 600 metres

14th July, Nepal

I'm on Everest, Earth's highest mountain. I've seen blue sheep and wild goats grazing. Their hooves give them a good grip on steep slopes.

Wild goats grazing

These sheep are called blue sheep – but they are not actually blue!

ECO SUCCESS

In the mountains of Pakistan, snow leopards kill people's goats. Project Snow Leopard pays farmers for any goats they lose, so that they don't shoot the leopards.

Mountain life

There are different habitats in the mountain biome. This is because it gets colder the higher up the mountain you go.

High up the mountain, animals have thick, shaggy coats to keep them warm. Only a few grasses and low-growing flowers can survive the cold. The top of the mountain might have snow all-year round.

Wildlife on the lower slopes is the same as in the surrounding countryside.

The Aymara people (say eye-mah-rah) live in the Andes Mountains in South America. They weave beautiful cloth from alpaca wool. Alpaca fleece is warm and water-resistant.

The Aymara carry their babies in colourful slings.

PLEASED TO MEET YOU

Temperate grassland biome

Description:

Grassy, treeless plains that have cold winters and hot summers

21st July, Kazakhstan

I'm in the steppes – the temperate grassland biome that stretches across Europe and Asia. Summers are hot and dry, and winters are cold. Grasses cope in all weathers!

The steppes have herds of grass-eating saiga antelopes.

Kazakhs are people who live on the steppes. They travel from place to place, grazing their sheep, cattle and horses. Kazakh yurts (tents) are made of felt. This is pressed wool that comes from the sheep.

Kazakhs use trained eagles to hunt foxes and hares for fur.

PLEASED TO MEET YOU

Mediterranean scrub biome

Description:

Land that has low-growing shrubs and grasses, with hot, dry summers and cool, rainy winters

28th July, Spain

'Scrub' doesn't sound great, but wow! You should smell the thyme, rosemary and sage when the hot sun beats down.

ECO SUCCESS

The Iberian lynx was almost extinct in Spain and Portugal's scrub biome. The organisation Iberlince reintroduced the cat, and now its population is growing.

This biome suits lizards and snakes, which cannot make their own body heat.

Desert biome

Description:

Very dry places with less than 25 cm of rain a year

4th August, Niger

At first, I couldn't see any life in the Sahara Desert, but this hot, sandy biome has many animals, and even some plants. So far I've spotted ants, a scorpion and a snake!

These animals have adapted to live in the desert biome.

FENNEC FOX

Adapted to survive

○ has huge ears which allow body heat to escape

GILA WOODPECKER

Adapted to survive

○ nests in a safe, cool hole in a saguaro cactus

Desert life

Camels can go for a week or more without water.

Deserts are the driest places on Earth. Some are hot and sandy. Further from the **Equator**, deserts can be cold, with stones, rocks or snow.

ECO SUCCESS

Australia's Bilby Project is working to save native desert animals and plants. It is trying to protect the endangered greater bilby. This shy, nocturnal animal comes out at night and uses its snout to dig out bulbs, minibeasts and fungi.

Tropical grassland biome

Description:

Grassy plains, dotted with shrubs and trees, that have two seasons: hot and dry or hot and wet

12th August, Kenya

I've always dreamed of coming to the African savannah, and now I'm here. It's the dry season, and huge herds of zebras and wildebeest have come north to find grass to eat. Along their journey, they faced fierce predators – lions, leopards, cheetahs, hyenas and crocodiles!

In October when the rains come, the zebras and wildebeest will make the dangerous journey south again.

Giraffe

Wildebeest crossing a river

Tropical grassland life

The African savannah is a tropical grassland biome. It is near to the Equator and is hot all-year round. There are two seasons: wet and dry.

Like temperate grasslands, tropical grasslands are home to grazing animals and the predators that hunt them.

Tropical rainforest biome

Description:

Forests near the Equator that are hot and rainy all-year round

19th August, Brazil

I've come to the Amazon in South America. It's the largest tropical rainforest, and is home to a fifth of the world's plants and birds.

I've never seen so many amazing insects! My guide said there are more than 7000 butterfly species here, and one single tree can be a habitat for 700 species of beetle.

There's fruit all-year round for this toucan.

Monkeys have long arms, legs and tails for swinging from tree to tree.

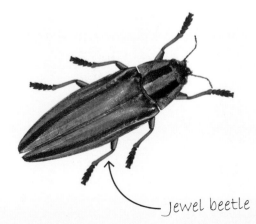

Jewel beetle

Tropical rainforest life

ECO SUCCESS

When rainforests are cleared to make way for farmland, mines and cities, animals lose their habitat. The organisation One Tree Planted raises money to plant new trees in the rainforest.

The Mbuti people live in West Africa's tropical rainforest. They hunt with bows, spears or nets, and collect fruits, nuts, leaves and honeycomb.

This man has a hunting net around his shoulders.

(P) PLEASED TO MEET YOU

Ocean biomes

26th August

The animals and plants in these biomes wouldn't last long away from the salty water. The conditions seem extreme to me – but that's because I'm adapted to live on land!

These are the four ocean biomes I'm visiting:

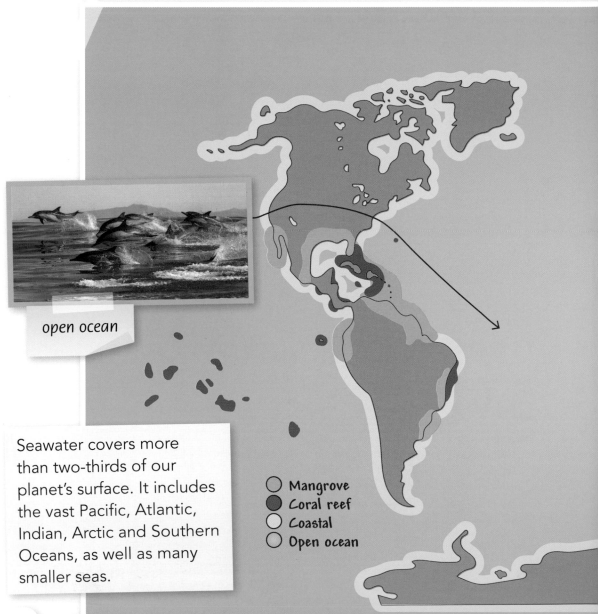

open ocean

Seawater covers more than two-thirds of our planet's surface. It includes the vast Pacific, Atlantic, Indian, Arctic and Southern Oceans, as well as many smaller seas.

○ Mangrove
● Coral reef
○ Coastal
○ Open ocean

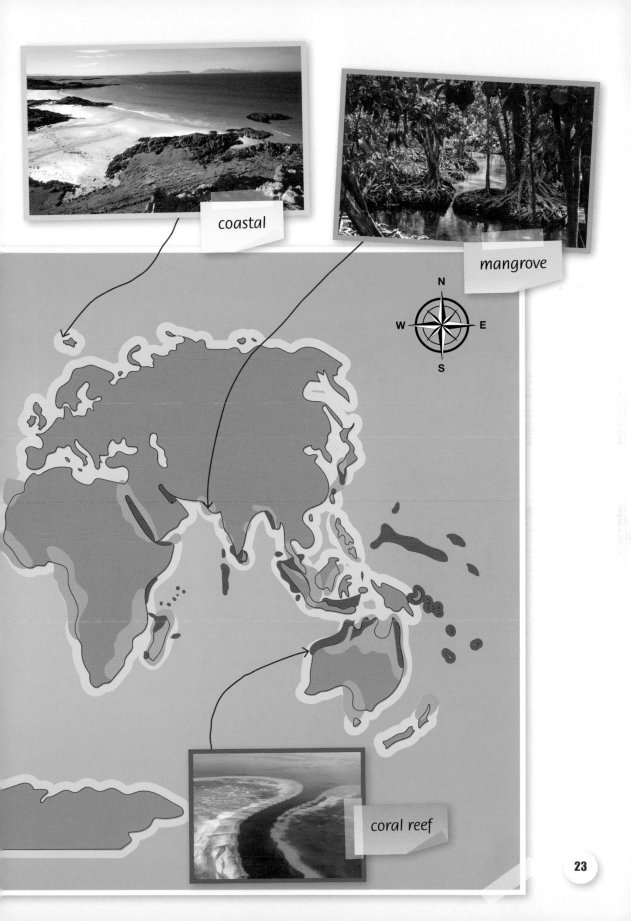

coastal

mangrove

coral reef

Coastal biome

Description:

Beaches and rocky shorelines at the edge of the ocean

4th September, UK

I'm in Scotland, at a coastal biome with rock pools and a sandy beach. Rock pool animals like this sea anemone have adapted to survive, whether their pool is dry or full of seawater.

TIDE IN. The sea anemone waves its tentacles to catch food.

TIDE OUT. The sea anemone tucks in its tentacles so they don't dry out.

Mangrove biome

Description:

Swampy 'forests' in hot parts of the world

12th September, Philippines

I'm in a special kind of wetland – a mangrove. Life here must cope with mud and tides of salty water. The roots of the trees are above the water so they can breathe air. It makes them look like they're on stilts!

These animals have adapted to survive in the mangrove biome.

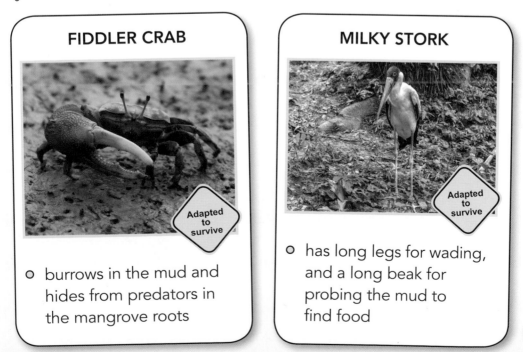

FIDDLER CRAB

Adapted to survive

o burrows in the mud and hides from predators in the mangrove roots

MILKY STORK

Adapted to survive

o has long legs for wading, and a long beak for probing the mud to find food

Coral reef biome

Description:

The most colourful biomes of all! A biome that forms around a rocky undersea structure built up from the remains of tiny animals called corals. The most colourful ones are in warmer, tropical waters.

20th September, Australia

Wow! I'm just back from diving along the Great Barrier Reef off Australia. It's magical! I saw a pram-sized clam and a giant jellyfish, blue starfish and purple sponges. I swam with angelfish and parrotfish.

ECO ALERT!

The Great Barrier Reef is the largest reef in the world, but it's in danger. Global warming is the worst threat because corals die if the water is too warm.

Some Polynesian people live on coral reef islands in the South Pacific. They fish and farm.

*Many Polynesian people build **outrigger canoes**.*

P

PLEASED TO MEET YOU

Coral reef life

As older coral dies, new corals grow on top.

The coral reef is a busy biome because it is home to a quarter of all marine life. The reef is made from the remains of billions of tiny animals called hard corals. The reef has soft corals too, which look more like plants. Both hard and soft corals form amazing shapes.

Corals are often different shapes. Look at these:

Bubble coral

Sea fan

Brain coral

Elkhorn coral

Violet coral

Open ocean biome

Description:

Deeper water, away from land

26th September, Atlantic Ocean

I'm in the open ocean biome. Seeing a pod of dolphins here is something I'll never forget. One calf swam so close to its mum, it seemed to be held by an invisible thread.

These animals have adapted to survive in the open ocean biome.

BARRACUDA

Adapted to survive

○ moves in a shoal (group) for safety from larger predators

GREAT WHITE SHARK

Adapted to survive

○ has a streamlined body to swim fast, and an incredible sense of smell for finding food

Ocean life

Life has adapted to live at different depths of the ocean – the sunlight, twilight and deep-sea biomes.

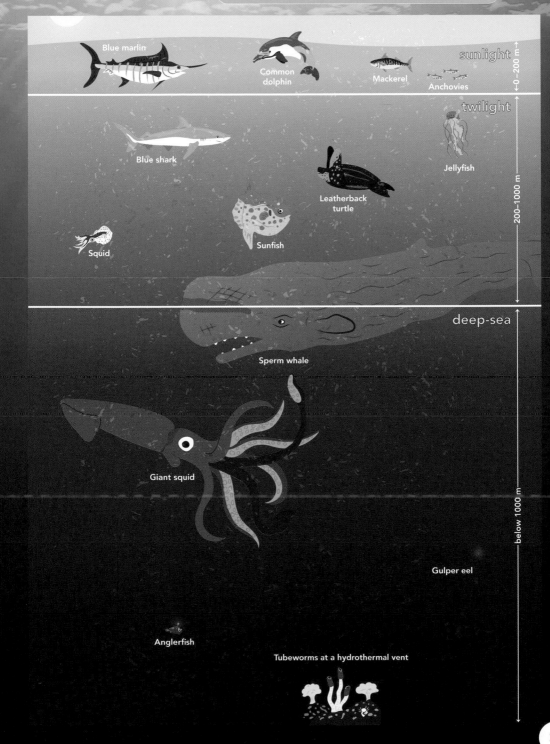

sunlight ← 0–200 m →

Blue marlin

Common dolphin

Mackerel

Anchovies

twilight

Blue shark

Jellyfish

Leatherback turtle

Squid

Sunfish

200–1000 m

deep-sea

Sperm whale

Giant squid

below 1000 m

Gulper eel

Anglerfish

Tubeworms at a hydrothermal vent

Deep-sea biome

Description:

The bottom layer of the open ocean biome that is below 1000 metres

5th October, Pacific Ocean

Only the tiniest fraction of the deep-sea biome has ever been explored. You can't dive here – you'd be crushed by the pressure of the water above you. You have to go down in a **submersible**.

No sunlight can reach this deep, so the water is cold and inky-black. It's hard to believe that any life survives here, but it does thanks to clever adaptations. Some creatures even make their own light.

The anglerfish has a glow-in-the-dark 'fishing rod' on its head. Smaller fish come close to see the light, and the anglerfish eats them.

This creature is just a mouth on a stalk! It's called a tunicate (say choo-nee-kay-t).

The dumbo octopus has fins above its eyes which let it hover above the ocean floor.

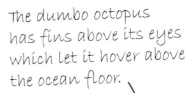

Ecosystems

Freshwater ecosystem

12th October, Australia

I've seen all of the land and sea biomes on my list — now for some smaller ecosystems!

Rivers, lakes, ponds and streams are freshwater ecosystems. They are found all over the world, in many different biomes. They're home to dragonflies, fish, frogs and ducks.

Dragonfly

Australian green and golden bell frog

ECO SUCCESS

In 2009, wild beavers were released into Scottish rivers after being extinct there for 500 years. Beavers might be introduced to other parts of the UK soon.

Wetland ecosystem

19th October, USA

Wetland ecosystems are a paradise for birdwatchers. I'm visiting wetlands in Florida. Herons, geese, cranes, pelicans and spoonbills all live here, or pass through. They usually have long legs so that they can wade through shallow waters, and they feed on plants, insects, frogs and fish.

Rosette spoonbill

The Bininj/Mungguy are Aboriginal Australians. They've lived in the wetlands of northern Australia for 40,000 years. Today the Bininj/Mungguy's wetland home is a national park. The people guide visitors around the park.

A Bininj/Mungguy rock painting of a fish.

PLEASED TO MEET YOU

33

Cave ecosystem

26th October, Slovenia

I love dark, echoey caves and the animals that live in them.
I'm not so keen on the smell of guano (bat poo), though!

Most caves form in soft, chalky rock. As water drips through the rock, it wears away, leaving underground hollows.

These animals have adapted to survive in cave ecosystems.

CAVE FISH

Adapted to survive

o is blind but can detect movement in the water

PIPISTRELLE BAT

Adapted to survive

o finds objects by echolocation – it listens to how its squeaks bounce back

Town and city ecosystem

1st November, Canada

In my travels I've encountered lots of wildlife out in the wilds, but what about the animals and plants that live alongside us? Towns and cities are ecosystems, too! They are found in different biomes all over the world. Plants push through paving slabs, and foxes and rats raid our rubbish.

Pigeons live in towns and cities all over the world.

Cockroaches live in most environments, even our homes. Yuck!

People in the Ethiopian city of Harar live alongside spotted hyenas. The predators roam inside the city walls, and locals feed them meat.

PLEASED TO MEET YOU

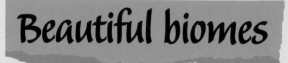

Beautiful biomes

30th November, Home

What an amazing journey! I can't decide which biome or ecosystem is my favourite. However, I do know one thing – I share this planet with living things that have adapted to survive in all sorts of environments.

TUNDRA BIOME

I've seen plants that grow in cold places ...

TROPICAL GRASSLAND BIOME

... in hot places ...

WETLAND ECOSYSTEM

... and in wet places.

CAVE ECOSYSTEM

And I've encountered animals that suit dark places ...

POLAR BIOME

... freezing-cold places ...

TEMPERATE WOODLAND BIOME

... cool, shady places ...

MOUNTAIN BIOME

... high places ...

CORAL REEF BIOME

... and even the salty sea!

Which biome did you like best?

Glossary

adapt to change to suit the surroundings

biome all the living things in a particular environment, such as a desert

climate zone a place that has particular weather conditions

ecosystem a community of life forms and their local environment

environment all the conditions that make a place what it is, including the weather and the landscape

Equator an imaginary line around the middle of the Earth that is an equal distance from each pole

global warming a rise in temperatures all around the world, caused by humans creating too many greenhouse gases, such as carbon dioxide and methane

habitat the place where an animal or plant lives

native naturally from a particular place

outrigger canoe a boat with a frame attached to one side to make it more stable in rough seas

predator an animal that hunts and eats other animals for food

submersible an underwater craft for one or two people

temperate from parts of the world where temperatures are not too hot and not too cold and there are usually four seasons

tropical from parts of the world close to the Equator where temperatures are hot and there are usually two seasons (wet or dry)

Index

Now answer the questions ...

1 What animals do Sami people keep?

2 Why does the brown bear hibernate in winter?

3 What does 'native' mean in the 'Eco Success' section on page 17?

4 Approximately how many butterfly species live in the rainforest?

5 What links the 'Eco Alert!' boxes on page 6 and page 26?

6 What kind of information do the 'Pleased to Meet You' boxes give? Why do you think the author included them?

7 'Seeing a pod of dolphins here is something I'll never forget.' What does 'pod' mean in this sentence?

8 Why might spotted hyenas choose to live in the city of Harar rather than the countryside?

9 Choose one of the biomes. How do you think it might change in the future, and why?

10 Which biome would you most like to visit, and why?